# PENCIL Play 2

Word Games, Picture Puzzles, Mazes, and More!

American Girl®

Published by Pleasant Company Publications

Visit our Web site at **americangirl.com**.

Printed in China
05 06 07 08 09 10 C&C 10 9 8 7 6 5 4 3 2

American Girl®, Addy®, Felicity®, Josefina®, Kaya®,
Kirsten®, Kit®, Molly®, Nellie™, and Samantha™
are trademarks of American Girl, LLC.

Questions or comments?
Call 1-800-845-0005, visit **americangirl.com**, or write to:
American Girl, P.O. Box 620497, Middleton, WI 53562-0497.

Written by Teri Witkowski
Art directed and designed by Cesca Piuma
Produced by Paula Moon-Bailey, Mary Cudnohfsky,
Judith Lary, and Dana Hoberg

Illustrations by Dan Andreasen, Nick Backes, Bill Farnsworth,
Renée Graef, Susan McAliley, Susan Moore, Lisa Pfeiffer, John Pugh,
Walter Rane, Dahl Taylor, Jean-Paul Tibbles, and Mike Wimmer

# Contents

**Picture Puzzles**

| | |
|---|---|
| Family Portraits | 1 |
| Inside the Rancho | 4 |
| Newsroom Knowledge | 14 |
| Kitchen Quiz | 24 |
| Patchwork Pictures | 31 |
| Where Did I See That? | 53 |

**Word Searches**

| | |
|---|---|
| All Dressed Up | 3 |
| City Search | 20 |
| Mr. Merriman's Shop | 36 |
| Kaya's World | 42 |
| Camp Gowonagin | 44 |

**Mazes**

| | |
|---|---|
| King's Creek Maze | 6 |
| Molly's Maze | 12 |
| Adventures at Piney Point | 38 |

**Crossword Puzzles**

| | |
|---|---|
| Kirsten's Crossword | 8 |
| Oh, Brothers! | 18 |
| Holiday Hobbies | 32 |
| Miss Victory | 40 |
| School Crossword | 50 |

**Codes**

| | |
|---|---|
| Celilo Falls | 23 |
| Party Problem | 27 |
| Confused Keys | 34 |
| Perfect Pets | 46 |
| Baby Britta | 52 |

**Word Games**

| | |
|---|---|
| Riding the Rails | 2 |
| Wise Words | 7 |
| Addy's Important Letter | 10 |
| Sister Scramble | 13 |
| Kirsten's New Name | 16 |
| The Dancing Lesson | 17 |
| A Surprise Friend | 22 |
| Sweet Sombrita | 26 |
| Penny Pincher Puzzle | 28 |
| Kaya Learns a Lesson | 30 |
| Treasures to Trade | 39 |
| Help for Josefina | 45 |
| Addy's Special Day | 48 |
| Kit's Cross-Out | 49 |

| | |
|---|---|
| **Answers** | 54 |

# Family Portraits

Draw a line from each American Girl to the grown-up who cared for her.

# Riding the Rails

Kit was eager for adventure the summer she met Will Shepherd, a young hobo from Texas. Will traveled the country for free by jumping into empty boxcars and riding the rails. Longing for excitement, Kit tried to hop a freight, too. To find out what happened to her, change each letter to the one that comes before it in the alphabet.

Tif hpu dbvhiu boe xbt ublfo up kbjm.

___  ___  ___  ___  ___  ___  ___  ___  ___  ___  ___  ___

___  ___  ___  ___  ___  ___  ___  ___  ___

# All Dressed Up

Samantha would never just tumble out of bed and arrive at the breakfast table in her pajamas. She followed the steps below to put on many layers of clothes, even in the summer! Can you find the underlined words hidden in the puzzle? They may be shown backward, forward, diagonally, or up and down.

1. A long frilly undershirt called a <u>chemise</u>

2. A pair of lace-trimmed <u>drawers</u>, or underpants

3. At least one lacy <u>petticoat</u>

4. Long cotton or woolen <u>stockings</u>

5. <u>Garters</u> to hold up the stockings

6. A fancy ruffled <u>dress</u>

7. High-buttoned <u>shoes</u>

8. A starched white <u>pinafore</u>

9. A fluffy <u>hairbow</u>

10. <u>Long underwear</u> in the winter

```
S J Q Q L C P Q B R P B R G H
S D K L N V I V E I N A R A A
E Y J K Q H G K N U E Q V R I
R X Y P A T W A G W T W Z T R
D S D A D Q F A R E A A N E B
S J T E K O Z E W S O G B R O
Z O J O R E D K D I C E D S W
I S C E C N U R E M I Z E P F
U D P P U K A U Z E T P G F Z
H I N G S W I H U H T Y U R G
T U N H E P Y N L C E R L I X
T O O R Z O Y R G G P E G P K
L E S O I X E W K S Z H X J G
S D J Y Q Z F N X D B H T K B
J T Y E X Q H O A Z M J I Y W
```

# *I*nside the Rancho

The house on the Montoya family *rancho*, or farm, was built around a center courtyard. Josefina and her sisters did most of their household chores in the courtyard, or *placita* (plah-SEE-tah), but the rooms inside the house were busy, too. See what you can find in this picture.

1. How many ladders can you find?

2. The hanging light is called an *araña* (ah-RAH-nya), which is the Spanish word for "spider." It's called an araña because it dangles from the ceiling like a spider. Where is it?

3. There are 12 candles in the araña. Can you find 12 more?

4. Josefina's family wove colorful rugs from the wool of the rancho's sheep. Seven of the rugs are rolled up in this picture. Can you find them?

5. Find two brooms.

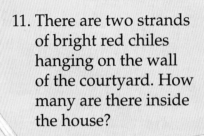

11. There are two strands of bright red chiles hanging on the wall of the courtyard. How many are there inside the house?

10. Where is the cat?

9. Faith was a very important part of Josefina's life. Her home included an altar where the family prayed each morning, noon, and evening. The altar is covered with a white cloth decorated with red thread. Find another white cloth with red thread.

7. Find two stools.

6. There is one wooden barrel in the courtyard. How many others can you find?

8. There were not a lot of chairs in Josefina's house. Instead, *bancos*, or low benches, were built into the walls. How many are there?

# King's Creek Maze

Felicity spent every summer at King's Creek Plantation, her grandfather's home on the York River in Virginia. Felicity and Grandfather began each day with a horseback ride around the plantation. Find the path that leads them from the stables to the river. (Hint: There's more than one!)

# Wise Words

Kaya befriended a lone dog that was starving and about to have pups. Kaya told her grandmother that the dog often seemed to be talking to her with its eyes. Kaya's grandmother agreed that animals talk to people in many ways. What else did she tell Kaya? To find out, cross out all the Ps, Ns, Bs, and Ks in the puzzle below. Then write the remaining letters in the spaces at the bottom of the page.

```
P A N B L K N K P L B C R
B K N E B N P B A K T K B
P N U B K R N P B K E P K
B N S H K B A N K B V N B
K E P W N P K I N B S D P
K B O N P M K T P B N O S
K N H B K A N R P P K E B
W N I K B T K H U N B K S
```

___ ___ ___   ___ ___ ___ ___ ___ ___ ___ ___

___ ___ ___ ___   ___ ___ ___ ___ ___ ___

___ ___ ___ ___ ___   ___ ___ ___ ___

# Kirsten's Crossword

Kirsten was eager for Papa to pick up the trunks they had to leave at Mr. Berkhoff's store when they arrived in Minnesota. When Papa finally had time, he let Kirsten go with him. Find out what happened on their adventure by completing the puzzle. If you need a hint, check the word list.

## Down

1. On the way to town, Papa and Kirsten sang Christmas _____.
3. In the middle of the storm, Kirsten found a ____ where she and Papa could wait for the snow to stop.
5. At the General Store, Mr. Berkhoff gave Kirsten a piece of cinnamon _____ from one of the glass jars on the counter.
7. The harness ____ on the horse's neck jingled merrily.
10. Papa wanted to hurry home because it was _____ harder.

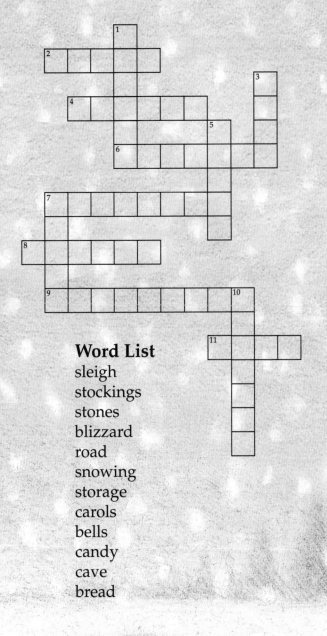

## Across

2. Kirsten gave Mr. Berkhoff a loaf of _____ and wished him a happy Christmas.
4. Mama heated _____ in the oven. They would keep Kirsten's and Papa's feet warm on the way to Maryville.
6. The Larsons' trunks were in a big _____ room at the back of the store.
7. Kirsten was worried they would lose their way in the _____ on the way home.
8. There was too much snow for the wagon, so Papa and Kirsten took the _____ to town.
9. Kirsten dressed in her warmest clothes and put on two pairs of wool _____.
11. There was so much snow on the way home that Papa couldn't see the _____.

**Word List**

sleigh
stockings
stones
blizzard
road
snowing
storage
carols
bells
candy
cave
bread

# Addy's Important Letter

After the war ended, Addy and her parents were determined to reunite their family in Philadelphia. Addy wrote letters to the Freedmen's Bureau asking for information about Sam, Esther, Uncle Solomon, and Auntie Lula. Help Addy finish her letter. First, unscramble the words in the list. Then find the right place for each of them in the letter.

BUAOT

ELVO

MUSRME

NEUJ

EERSTT

PLEH

TWIRE

AYRES

MALIFY

WNKO

YABB

SIMLE

NFDI

_____ 9, 1865

Dear Friends,

Can you _____ us find our _____? Please. Solomon and Lula Morgan. They caring for our dear _____ Esther Walker. We last seen them last _____ on the plantation belonging to Master Stevens. The plantation is some twenty _____ north of Raleigh. We need information _____ Samuel Walker also. He about 17 _____ old. He was sold from the Stevens plantation last summer. We don't _____ where he was sold to. If you can help us, _____ to Ben Walker on South _____ in Philadelphia, Penn. We want to _____ them very much because we ___ them all.

Ben Walker

# Molly's Maze

Molly, Linda, and Susan collected bottle tops for their school's Lend-a-Hand project. Find the neighborhood path that has the most bottle tops.

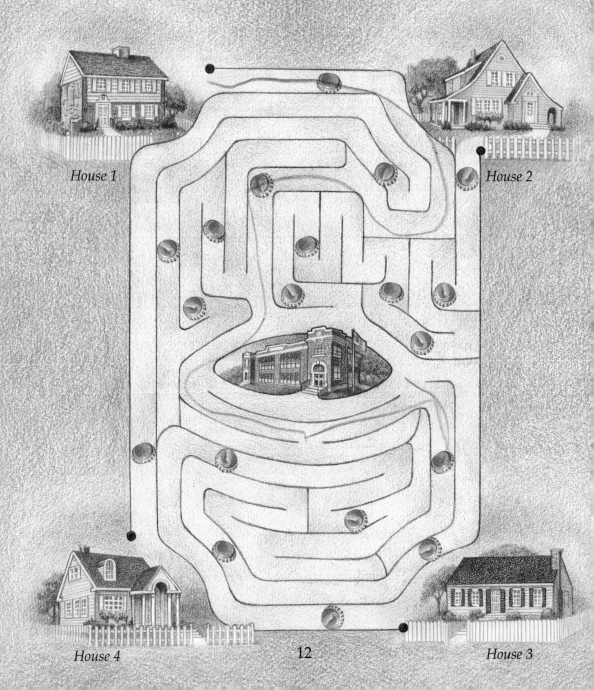

*House 1*

*House 2*

*House 4*

12

*House 3*

# Sister Scramble

Samantha was thrilled when Uncle Gard and Aunt Cornelia adopted Nellie and her little sisters, Jenny and Bridget. At last Samantha had sisters of her very own! Below is a list of some of the things that the girls did together, but parts of the words are missing. Find the letters that complete the names of the things that the girls enjoyed.

1. Samantha told Bridget and Jenny st_ _ _ es while they took their bath.
2. After dinner everyone sat in the p_ _ _or with Uncle Gard and Aunt Cornelia.
3. Samantha and Nellie went to sc_ _ _l together.
4. All the girls loved to take a ride in Uncle Gard's m_ _ _ rcar.
5. Before they fell asleep in the bedroom they shared, Samantha and Nellie whispered and _ _ _ gled about the day.
6. Samantha cut out paper _ _ _ ls for Jenny and Bridget to play with.
7. Everyone liked to go to the ice c_ _ _m parlor.
8. Samantha and Nellie took Bridget and Jenny for walks in the p_ _ _.
9. Most of all, Samantha and Nellie loved to _ _ _k to each other about their hopes and dreams.

arl

dol

ori

ark

oto

gig

rea    tal    hoo

13

# Newsroom Knowledge

Study the details of the newsroom for several minutes, then turn
the page to see how much you remember about the picture.

# Newsroom Knowledge (continued)

Don't read this until you have read page 15!

Do you have a reporter's eye for detail? Answer the questions to find out. No peeking!

1. Besides Kit, how many people were in the room?
2. The name of the newspaper was on the door.
   Circle the correct name.
   The Cincinnati Herald
   The Cincinnati Enquirer
   The Cincinnati Register
3. How many people were wearing glasses?
4. What month was on the calendar?
5. What was the color of the woman's shirt?
6. Which president was on the poster on the wall?
7. How many typewriters were there?

# Kirsten's New Name

Kirsten became friends with an Indian girl named Singing Bird. What did Singing Bird call Kirsten? To find out, cross out all the letters that appear three times. Then write the remaining letters in the spaces below.

Y S C Q N E J
Q N L L T C O
W S T N H C J
Q A J S I T R

___ ___ ___ ___ ___   ___ ___ ___ ___

# The Dancing Lesson

Felicity was delighted to receive an invitation to a dancing lesson at the royal Governor's Palace. Unscramble the words to see all Felicity had to do to prepare for the grand event. If you get stuck, check the word list.

1. First, Felicity had to ask her **rahfet** for permission to attend the lesson. _father_
2. At Miss Manderly's the girls practiced making a **ystruc**. _curtsy_
3. Felicity's mother agreed to sew a beautiful new **nowg** for her. _gown_
4. Because she was not a very good dancer, Felicity had to **riccepat** her steps. _____
5. Felicity took a hot **hbta** and used her mother's very best soap. _____
6. Nan **shubrde** Felicity's hair until it was smooth and shiny. _____
7. Her mother let Felicity wear one of her best pearl **graniesr** on a cord around her neck. _____
8. It wasn't proper for Felicity to arrive at the palace alone, so Ben agreed to **tecros** her. _____
9. Felicity used her very best **nemnars** when she met the governor and his wife. _____

**Word List**
gown
earrings
brushed
father
manners
escort
curtsy
bath
practice

17

# Oh, Brothers!

Some had big ones. Some had little ones. Some had both! Brothers were part of the family for Kit, Addy, Felicity, Kirsten, and Molly. Complete the crossword to discover the fun—and frustration—brothers could bring. If you need a hint, check the word list.

## Down

1. In Philadelphia, Addy and Sam went to several _____ looking for Esther, Auntie Lula, and Uncle Solomon.
3. Kit hated it when her brother called her _____.
7. Addy's big brother Sam liked to tell her stories and ask her _____ .
8. Molly called her 12-year-old brother Ricky a _____ because he was always teasing her.

## Across

2. Charlie was the one who told Kit their father's car dealership was going out of _____ because of the Depression.
4. Felicity took William and Nan to the tannery to see Penny. Their visit was supposed to be a secret, but William gave it away at _____.
5. Molly and Ricky loved to bring the Christmas _____ up from the basement together.
6. Her brother Lars let Kirsten go trapping with him because she knew the _____ so well.
9. While Felicity's mother worked on the gown for the ball, Felicity _____ with William.
10. Kirsten wanted to surprise her parents with honey, so she made Peter promise not to tell anyone about the ___ tree she'd found.

18

## Word List

rat
hospitals
suppertime
riddles
played
ornaments
business
squirt
forest
bee

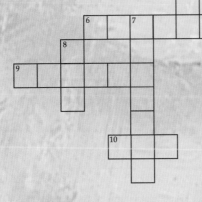

19

# City Search

When Addy and her momma arrived in Philadelphia, they had to get used to living in a big city. The names of the places they soon became familiar with are hidden in the puzzle below. The underlined words may be shown forward, backward, diagonally, or up and down. Some of the letters will be used for more than one word.

1. Addy and Momma arrived on <u>pier three</u> on a hot August day.

2. Momma got a job at Mrs. Ford's <u>dress shop</u>.

3. Addy and Momma lived in the <u>garret</u> room above Mrs. Ford's shop.

4. Addy was nervous her first day at the Sixth Street <u>School</u>.

5. Addy and Momma bought some of the things they needed at Mr. Delmonte's <u>secondhand shop</u>.

6. Addy often made deliveries to Mrs. Ford's wealthy customers on <u>Society Hill</u>.

7. Momma told Addy to be careful crossing the busy <u>streets</u> of the city.

8. After Poppa joined Addy and Momma in Philadelphia, they moved into a <u>boarding house</u>.

9. Addy and Sarah walked to the <u>drugstore</u> to get medicine for M'dear.

10. When her friend had to stay home from school, Addy went to <u>Sarah's house</u> and helped her with the day's lessons.

11. Hoping to find the rest of her family, Addy wrote letters and dropped them off at the Quaker <u>Aid Society</u>.

12. Sam and Addy went to the <u>City Hospital</u> looking for Auntie Lula and Uncle Solomon.

13. Addy often passed the <u>Institute</u> for Colored Youth, where she hoped to someday study to be a teacher.

S A L O C A Z G U P Y S Y B P
M E I L Z F G N O F T P T O I
D B C I I G B H F R P C E A E
L R Y O O H S S E Y I H I R R
L X U I N S Y E P T T C C D T
O O T G S D T T Y P G R O I H
S J O E S S H H E U V U S N R
U A R H N T O A A I K H D G E
V D D I C S O J N Q C C I H E
A E Q L P S U R E D W O A O L
Z J A I V Q G E E I S K S U J
U S T U T E R R A G V H G S R
Q A I N S T I T U T E O O E G
L E S U O H S H A R A S T P Y
C I V Y M I S E O C U E H X F

# *A* Surprise Friend

When it was time for Felicity's horse to have her foal, Penny was having trouble. She needed help, but Felicity's father was not home. There was only one person who could help Penny, and it was someone Felicity hadn't always trusted. Who was it? To find out, cross out all the letters that appear three times. Then write the remaining letters in the spaces below.

J A O I P D Q K
R S Q R G O A S
G K Y A K S R N
D Q Y E P P O D

\_ \_ \_ \_ \_ \_ \_

# Celilo Falls

Each summer Kaya and her people traveled to Celilo Falls where thousands of other Indian families and friends gathered for salmon fishing. It was a festive time with much fun and celebrating. Use the code to discover the activities Kaya loved to take part in.

1. 18-11-9-2-25-5-10     — — — — — — —
2. 10-9-17-6-21     — — — — —
3. 2-9-5-24-25-5-10     — — — — — — —
4. 11-9-24-6-21     — — — — —
5. 7-9-11-9-2-6-21     — — — — — — —
6. 15-6-9-21-18-25-5-10     — — — — — — — —

| | | | | | |
|---|---|---|---|---|---|
| 1-H | 2-D | 3-K | 4-U | 5-N | 6-E |
| 7-P | 8-X | 9-A | 10-G | 11-R | 12-J |
| 13-B | 14-O | 15-F | 16-W | 17-M | 18-T |
| 19-Z | 20-Y | 21-S | 22-L | 23-Q | 24-C |
| | | 25-I | 26-V | | |

# Kitchen Quiz

Study Molly's kitchen for several minutes,
then turn the page to test your memory.

# Kitchen Quiz (continued)

Don't read this until you have read page 25!
Circle the items you saw in Molly's kitchen.
No peeking!

| | | |
|---|---|---|
| sugar canister | table | plants |
| pot holders | mixer | garbage can |
| microwave | blender | fruit |
| teakettle | rug | loaf of bread |
| coffee cups | clock | cookbooks |
| cookie jar | blue plates | dishwasher |

# Sweet Sombrita

Josefina named her baby goat Sombrita because it followed her everywhere. What does *sombrita* mean in Spanish? Fill in the missing vowels to find out.

L_ttl_ Sh_d_w

# Party Problem

What happened that made Samantha and her birthday guests look so unhappy? Use the American Girl Code to find out.

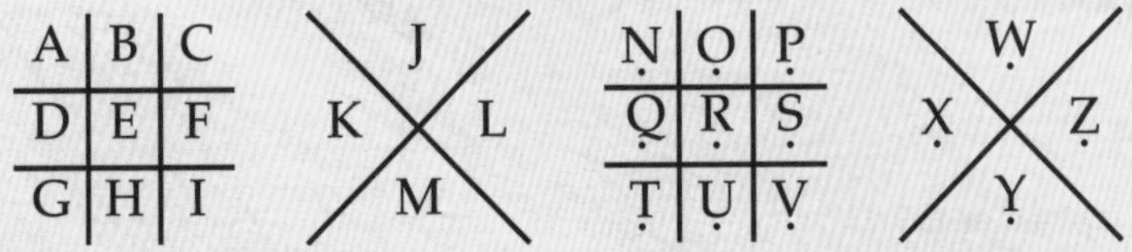
A B C
D E F
G H I
J
K L
M
N O P
Q R S
T U V
W
X Z
Y

# $\mathscr{P}$enny Pincher Puzzle

At first, Kit didn't like Aunt Millie's idea of a Penny Pincher birthday party. Kit was embarrassed about the things her family did at home to save money, and she didn't want her friends to know how poor they were. But Kit realized her aunt's ideas were clever— and fun—ways to make do during the Depression.

Unscramble the boldfaced words on the right to discover how Kit and her guests celebrated at the Penny Pincher Party. Then arrange the letters that appear in the circles to reveal one of Aunt Millie's favorite sayings.

1. TAYRP TSHA

2. ELDDIF

3. NCADE

4. LADRIGN

5. RAACEM

6. TOH SODG

7. SEACELKNC

8. DINNODLEA

9. GEGS

10. NATNLRES

W _ T _ N _ , W _ _ _ O _ .

1. Stirling made paper **tayrp tsha** for all the guests to wear.

2. Mr. Peck played his big bass **elddif**.

3. Mr. and Mrs. Bell taught everyone to square **ncade**.

4. Miss Hart and Miss Finney sang "My **ladrign** Clementine."

5. Charlie took pictures with his **raacem**.

6. Aunt Millie's friend the butcher helped them cook **toh sodg** on sticks over a fire.

7. Kit's mother taught them how to make flower **seacelknc**.

8. Aunt Millie showed everyone how to pick **dinnodlea** greens to make a salad.

9. Kit's friends fed the chickens and gathered **gegs**.

10. The yard was lit with **natnlres** Aunt Millie had saved from a trash pile.

# *K*aya Learns a Lesson

Kaya's father was an expert horseman, and Kaya often went to him for advice. He told her no one is born knowing how to ride. What else did he tell her? Solve the puzzle below by deciding which letter goes into which box in each column. A letter can be used only once. Leave the dark blue boxes empty.

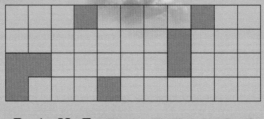

```
R A H E E A T D I O O
Y E S P R S I E T H E
O R O H C E   Y N G .
U     R V     T U
```

# Patchwork Pictures

Kirsten and her friends loved working on their quilt together.
Find the two pictures that are exactly alike.

# Holiday Hobbies

13. In America, Kirsten celebrated the day the Declaration of _____ was signed on the fourth of July.
16. Christmas was Molly's dad's favorite time of year, and he made sure it was full of _____.

## Down

1. Samantha looked forward to decorating a _____ house every year at Christmas.
3. Each _____, Molly and her friends tried to come up with the most creative costume.
5. Felicity, Nan, and William loved play with the wooden ark. It was special _____ that was brought out at only Christmastide.
8. Summer salmon _____ at Celilo Falls was the most festive time of year for Kaya's people.
9. Samantha didn't buy most of her Christmas gifts. She had fun ___ them instead.

## Across

2. As Christmas approached, Felicity's mother _____ their home with holly berries.
4. Josefina celebrated her birthday on the feast day of _____ Joseph.
6. On the last day of the _____, Addy's family went to church for the Emancipation Celebration, where Addy read the Proclamation about freedom.
7. Addy's momma made _____ potato pudding every Christmas.
10. Molly thought the best part about Halloween was going _____-or-treating.
11. At school, Kit's class created the scenery for the Thanksgiving _____.

12. Kit's favorite tradition was having waffles for _____ next to the tree on Christmas Eve.
14. Kirsten's whole family went to Maryville to watch the big Fourth of July _____.
15. Every Christmas, Josefina's mamá made a new _____ for the doll Josefina's sisters shared.

**Word List**
gingerbread
trick
dinner
Halloween
fishing
toy
Saint
dress
pageant
decorated
surprises
year
Independence
parade
sweet
making

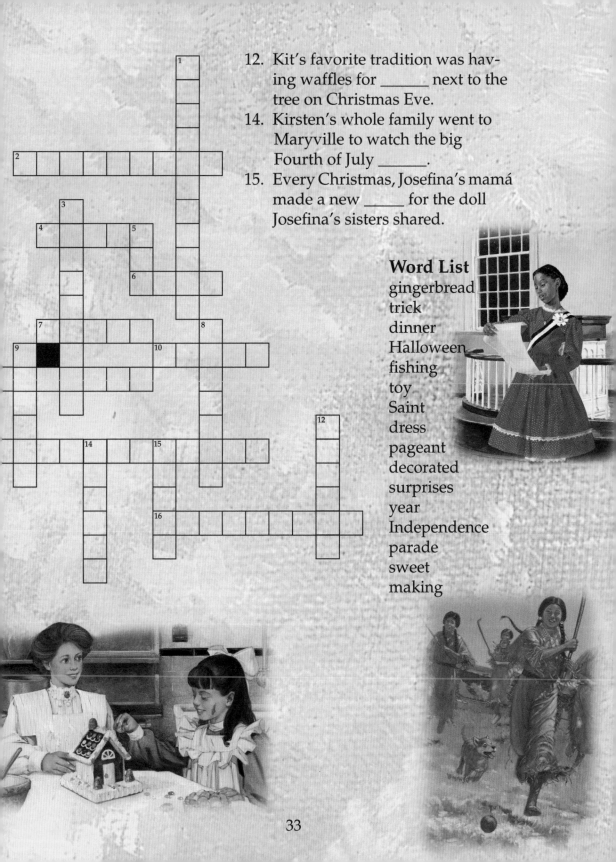

# Confused Keys

Some of the keys on Kit's typewriter are broken. The Os look like Us and the Es look like Os. The S doesn't work at all! Can you fix the mistakes in Kit's newspaper?

# The Hard Times News

```
*********************************************
```

Oditor: Kit Kittrodgo

Arti_t:_tirling Huward

Advi_ur: Magirx Margarot Kittrodgo

### *WANTOD*

Tall boardod man tu _haro _looping
purch with oarly-ri_ing, agrooablo
toonagor. Mu_t play duublo ba__ and
drink cuffoo. Call Charlio Kittrodgo.

 *WANTOD*

Du yuu havo intoro_ting, oxciting _turio_
tu toll abuut advonturo_ in nur_ing? If
_u, I'd liko tu hoar thom.

### *WANTOD IMMODIATOLY*

Talontod handyman tu fix _looping purch
_u it will _loop twu. Groat wurking
cunditiun_! Call tho Kittrodgo family.

### *WANTOD*

Noat and tidy lady tu holp with huu_o-
kooping in oxchango fur ruum and buard.
Call Margarot Kittrodgo.

### *WANTOD*

Kid with wagun tu haul away
loftuvor lumbor _uitablo fur u_o in fixing _looping purch. Call Ruthio _mithon_.

Mr. Merriman's Shop

Felicity thought her father's shop was the finest store in all of Williamsburg. The shelves were filled with useful items, and Felicity loved to daydream about the faraway places everything came from. The names of some of those items are hidden in the puzzle. They may be shown forward, backward, diagonally, or up and down. Some of the letters will be used for more than one word.

| | | |
|---|---|---|
| apron | dishes | rake |
| baskets | fabric | ribbon |
| books | fishing hook | rice |
| candles | flour | soap |
| candy | kettles | spices |
| coffee | nails | tea |
| comb | nightcap | yarn |

```
P Q A G R A P W C B F U K N Y G X D
B A S K E T S O C L M O X O N S G L
S O A P S Y F W O I O O O B K Y K T
E N X E B F A U H R K C B T Z E S
K B C M E D R R G D F B T I I V T Q
A I L E R O C N N B H Y A R V O T Z
R I E C H O I R N O O G J F H Z L Y
N L S C A H S L I A N O E F C J E R
C T N D S N S E H S I D K N A K S R
O P G I J K D R J X B D E S N L Y E
E I F V G P Z L A P R O N S D T B Y
A F C X K H R L E G W R P S Y E N Z
V M C A N H T Q K S Y I E T G A Z M
S S V M F X D C X L C C J I T S S R
S C X G Q P Z P A E I L Q F H Y Z T
Z Y X N H R D R S P P A K O R C K Z
```

# Adventures at Piney Point

Summers were full of adventure at Grandmary's home in the mountains. Samantha loved to fill her pack basket with sandwiches and butterfly nets and go exploring. Help Samantha get to the waterfall on Teardrop Island without getting stuck on the rocks.

# Treasures to Trade

When the wagon train of American traders arrived in Santa Fe, Josefina and her sisters each had a blanket to trade for anything they wanted.

To reveal what Francisca chose, change each letter to the one that comes before it in the alphabet.

b njssps

_ _ _ _ _ _ _

To find out what Clara wanted, change each letter to the one that comes after it in the alphabet.

jmhsshmf mddckdr

_ _ _ _ _ _ _ _ _ _ _ _ _ _ _

To discover what Josefina admired, change each letter to the one that comes before it in the alphabet.

b upz gbsn

a _ _ _ _ _ _ _
a toy farm

39

# Miss Victory

More than anything, Molly wanted to dance the part of Miss Victory in the Red Cross show. Complete the puzzle to discover the details. If you need help, check the word list.

## Down

1. The Miss Victory dance was the grand finale because it was the _____ act of the show.

2. The girl who was chosen for Miss Victory got to carry the costume home in a special plaid _____.

3. The best news was that Molly's _____ would be home to see the show.

4. When it was her turn to try out, Molly took off her _____ so she would look more sophisticated.

5. Nearly everyone in town was taking part in the big "_____ for the U.S.A." show.

7. Before she tried out for Miss Victory, Molly wanted to get a permanent wave so her hair would be _____.

8. Linda and Susan gave Molly their _____ money for the permanent wave kit.

10. Molly's mom was in the show, too. She was giving a _____ about the Red Cross Blood Drive.

11. Everyone in Miss LaVonda's class got to try out for the part of Miss Victory, who had a _____ dance.

## Across

2. The Miss Victory dance got a _____ ovation.
6. Molly, Linda, and Susan took ___ dance lessons with Miss LaVonda, who was in charge of the show.
7. Molly loved the _____ Miss Victory got to wear.
9. The day before the show, everyone attended a dress _____.
11. Jill offered to set Molly's hair in pin curls before she went to _____ so she would wake up with wavy hair.
12. Molly danced in perfect time to the music and everyone _____ she should be Miss Victory.

## Word List

hurray
tap
solo
costume
curly
movie
dad
sleep
glasses
standing
agreed
suitcase
rehearsal
speech
last

# Kaya's World

In 1764, Kaya's people got everything they needed from the natural world around them. Their food, clothing, and shelter came from the earth, the sky, the seas and rivers, and their fellow creatures in nature. Some of the items Kaya used are hidden in the puzzle. The underlined words may be shown forward, backward, diagonally, or up and down. Some of the letters will be used for more than one word.

1. Every morning at dawn—in cold weather and in warm—Kaya went to the <u>river</u> to bathe.
2. Kaya slept on a soft mattress of dried <u>grass</u> and bark.
3. Brown Deer swept the camp with a broom made of sage <u>branches</u>.
4. Women covered the tepees with mats woven from tule (TOO-lee) <u>reeds</u>.
5. Bear Blanket was a medicine woman who used <u>herbs</u> to heal sickness.
6. Men whittled <u>sticks</u> to make arrows.
7. Kaya used a box-turtle <u>shell</u> to hold green paint, which was made from river <u>algae</u>.
8. Women boiled water by dropping <u>stones</u> heated in a fire into a basket of water.
9. Aalah, Kaya's grandmother, taught her how to weave baskets and bags from <u>beargrass</u>.
10. Kaya's people traveled to Celilo Falls each summer to fish for <u>salmon</u>.
11. Kaya loved the delicious <u>huckleberries</u> that grew along the mountainsides.
12. Women and girls dug <u>camas roots</u>, which they ate raw or baked in underground ovens.
13. In the winter, Kaya wore a thick <u>buffalo</u> robe against the cold.
14. Elk <u>teeth</u> were the most prized decorations on clothing.
15. Speaking Rain wore a pretty necklace of white clamshell <u>beads</u>.

```
B E A R G R A S S R S Q S E R
B R E E D S H S E T E T H R E
L R I M A P A E I S O B E E V
N J A L W R V C R O V U L E I
Q O G N G S K N R B V F L D R
F A M O C S D S E P S F L I U
E Q F L M H A A B Z J A H L R
R M R R A M E P E H O L I H V
J X T Y A S G S L B Z O T Y S
C Y V C V A Y B K S E N O T S
H T E E T T H Z C O O I Z N B
T D B P Z E X N U G O K F Q D
X K L X C J Y F H Z X O B C J
```

# Camp Gowonagin

There was so much to do at Camp Gowonagin! Molly, Linda, and Susan learned something new every day. Circle the things the girls did at camp. The words may be shown backward, forward, diagonally, or up and down. Some of the letters will be used for more than one word.

Then write the remaining letters in order from left to right to discover one of Molly's favorite moments at camp.

ART PROJECTS    SING-ALONGS

CANOEING    SOFTBALL

WIENIE ROASTS    CAMPFIRES

CRAFTS    VOLLEYBALL

SWIMMING    BASKETBALL

NATURE HIKES    SAILING

TENNIS

```
W A S G N O L A G N I S
I V R S E R I F P M A C
E O B T C A N O E I N G
N L S A P S T F A R C L
I L W T S R H E E V E L
E E I N I K O N G F L A
R Y M A G L E J O W E B
O B M R I N G T E C E T
A A I R E M O N B C Y F
S L N S I N N E T A T O
T L G S A I L I N G L S
S E K I H E R U T A N L
```

_ _ _ _  _ _ _ _ _ _ _ _  _ _ _ _

_ _ _ _ _ _ _ _ _  _ _ _ _ _ _

# Help for Josefina

Tía Magdalena was Josefina's godmother, and she and Josefina had a very special bond. When Josefina was worried that Tía Dolores was going to leave the rancho, she went to Tía Magdalena for advice. What did Tía Magdalena tell her? Follow the instructions below, and then read the answer.

1. Cross out 2 colors.
2. Cross out 3 trees.
3. Cross out 4 words that rhyme with flower.
4. Cross out 3 kinds of corn.

| SWEET | DO | SOUR | YELLOW | NOT |
|--------|--------|---------|---------|--------|
| TOWER | MAPLE | LOSE | SHOWER | ELM |
| HOPE | POWER | POP | IN | YOUR |
| PURPLE | OAK | HEART'S | CARAMEL | DESIRE |

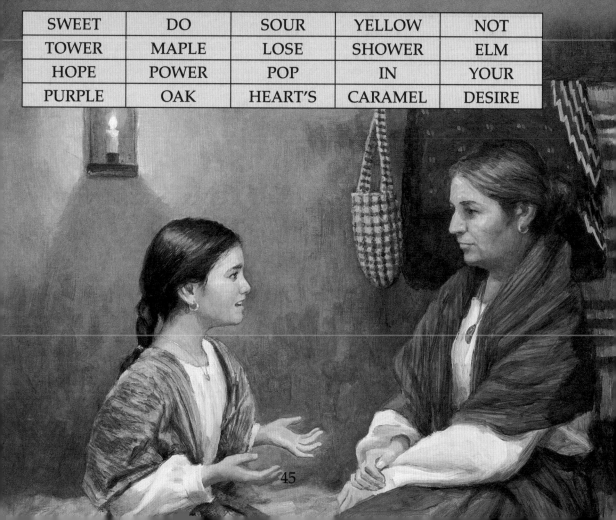

# Perfect Pets

Use the code to spell the name of the animal each American Girl adored.

1. It wasn't a dog or a cat or a horse that Josefina nursed to health.

2. Felicity named her horse after its bright copper coat.

3. Kirsten's pet had kittens.

4. Kit's dog was a basset hound.

5. Aunt Cornelia's puppy ran off with a teddy bear at Samantha's birthday party.

6. Addy loved to visit the bright yellow bird in M'Dear's room.

7. Kaya didn't choose her horse; her horse chose her.

8. There were two puppies at Molly's birthday party, and she got to keep one.

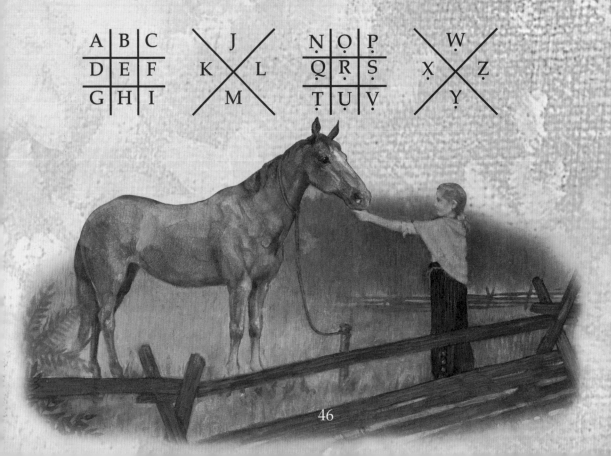

1. _____

5. ___

2. _____

6. _____

3. _____

7. _____ ____

4. ____

8. _____

47

# Addy's Special Day

Like many former slaves, Addy didn't know the exact date of her birthday. Instead, Addy got to choose a special day to claim for her birthday. To discover which day Addy chose and why it was so special, solve the puzzle below. You must decide which letter goes into which box in each column. A letter can be used only once. Leave the blue boxes empty.

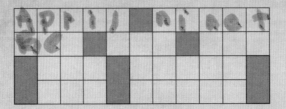

```
W A R R L C N D I L Y
A W H I T E N V N D H
  T A E     H E I D T
  P S       I   E A
```

# Kit's Cross-Out

Kit wrote a story about her best friend, Ruthie, and gave it to her for Christmas. What was the name of the story? Follow the instructions below, then read the answer.

1. Cross out 3 flowers.
2. Cross out 2 kinds of jewelry.
3. Cross out 3 boys' names.
4. Cross out 4 musical instruments.
5. Cross out 3 performers you'd see at the circus.

| ANDREW | FLUTE | THE | ROSE | ACROBAT |
|---|---|---|---|---|
| STORY | CLOWN | PIANO | OF | VIOLIN |
| RING | TULIP | BRACELET | GUITAR | MIKE |
| PRINCESS | MAGICIAN | CHARLIE | RUTHIE | DAFFODIL |

49

# School Crossword

Not all the American Girls went to school in classrooms. Felicity's lessons took place at the home of a respectable gentlewoman. Josefina learned to read and write at her family's rancho. Kaya's classroom was the world around her. Solve the puzzle to discover what learning was like for the American Girls. If you need a hint, check the word list.

**Across**

1. When Molly was called on in class, she stood next to her _____ to answer.
6. Kaya's grandparents were her main _____ because they had the most wisdom and experience.
9. During morning lessons, Samantha and her classmates left their lunchboxes in the _____ with their jackets.
10. Being educated as a gentlewoman meant Felicity had lessons in dancing, handwriting, fancy stitchery, and the proper way to serve _____.
12. Tía Dolores brought paper, pen, ink, and a _____ desk when she moved in with Josefina's family.

15. Kaya learned how to build her family's homes by making play _____.
16. Felicity was nervous about the lesson at the Governor's Palace because she wasn't very good at _____.

**Down**

2. Miss Campbell told Molly's class that being a go[od] _____ was as important as being a good sold[ier]
3. Stirling walked to the girls' side of the lunchroo[m] every day to get a sandwich from Kit because th[e] two of them shared a _____.

4. Kirsten was very nervous when she found out she'd have to memorize a poem and _____ it in front of the class.

5. Josefina wanted to learn how to read her mother's favorite prayers, poems, and _____ from the book Tía Dolores had written.

7. Addy studied very hard and won first prize in the _____ match.

8. During _____ class, Samantha practiced holding her pen properly and writing fancy letters.

11. Kirsten had to learn to speak English at school even though she spoke _____ at home.

13. The first word Addy learned to write was her _____.

14. When Kit was called on in _____ group, she didn't know what page they were on because she was busy thinking up better endings to the story.

**Word List**

writing
lunchbox
student
tepees
spelling
teachers
dancing
cloakroom
penmanship
desk
Swedish
reading
name
stories
tea
recite

# Baby Britta

After baby Britta was born, Mama needed Kirsten's help more than ever. Kirsten had to stay home from school to get all the chores done! Use the code to discover all that Kirsten did.

1. 16-9-21-1  2-25-9-7-6-11-21
   W a s h _ _ _ _ _ _ _

2. 24-14-14-3  2-25-5-5-6-11
   _ _ _ _  _ _ _ _ _ _

3. 10-9-18-1-6-11  6-10-10-21
   _ _ _ _ _ _  _ _ _ _

4. 17-25-22-3  24-14-16-21
   _ _ _ _  _ _ _ _

5. 24-1-4-11-5  13-4-18-18-6-11
   _ _ _ _ _  _ _ _ _ _ _

6. 7-25-24-3  13-6-11-11-25-6-21
   _ _ _ _  _ _ _ _ _ _ _

7. 15-6-6-2  18-1-6  24-1-25-24-3-6-5-21
   _ _ _ _  _ _ _  _ _ _ _ _ _ _ _

8. 17-9-3-6  24-22-14-18-1-6-21  15-14-11  18-1-6  13-9-13-20
   _ _ _ _  _ _ _ _ _ _ _  _ _ _  _ _ _  _ _ _ _

| | | | | |
|---|---|---|---|---|---|
| 1-H | 2-D | 3-K | 4-U | 5-N | 6-E |
| 7-P | 8-X | 9-A | 10-G | 11-R | 12-J |
| 13-B | 14-O | 15-F | 16-W | 17-M | 18-T |
| 19-Z | 20-Y | 21-S | 22-L | 23-Q | 24-C |
| | | 25-I | 26-V | | |

# Where Did I See That?

Each of these images is hidden somewhere in this book. Can you find them all? Write down the page numbers on which they appear.

1. Page _____

2. Page _____

3. Page _____

4. Page _____

5. Page _____

6. Page _____

7. Page _____

8. Page _____

# Answers

## Riding the Rails, page 2
She got caught and was taken to jail.

## All Dressed Up, page 3

```
S J Q Q L C P Q B R P B R G H
S D K L N V I V E I N A R A I
E Y J K Q H G K N U E Q V R R
R X Y P A T W A G W T W Z T B
D S D A D Q F A R E A A N E O
S J T E K O Z E W S O G B R W
Z O J O R E D K D I C E D S W
I S C E C N U R E M I Z E P F
U D P P U K A U Z E T P G F Z
H I N G S W I H U H T Y U R G
T U N H E P Y N L C E R L I X
T O O R Z O Y R G G P E G P K
L E S O I X E W K S Z H X J G
S D J Y Q Z F N X D B H T K B
J T Y E X Q H O A Z M J I Y W
```

## Inside the Rancho, page 4
1. 3
2. See illustration
3. See illustration
4. See illustration
5. See illustration
6. 5
7. See illustration
8. 4
9. See illustration
10. See illustration
11. 2

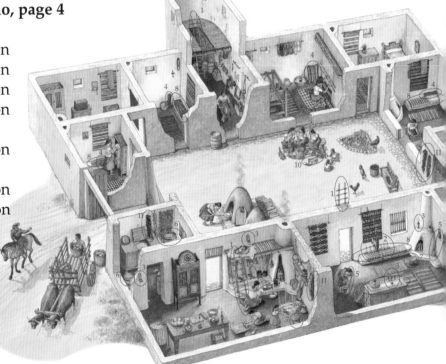

## King's Creek Maze, page 6

## Wise Words, page 7

All creatures have wisdom to share with us.

## Kirsten's Crossword, page 8

## Addy's Important Letter, page 10

| | | |
|---|---|---|
| June | miles | street |
| help | about | find |
| family | years | love |
| baby | know | |
| summer | write | |

## Molly's Maze, page 12

House 1.  Two bottlecaps
House 2.  Six bottlecaps
House 3.  Five bottlecaps
House 4.  Five bottlecaps

## Sister Scramble, page 13

| | | |
|---|---|---|
| 1. ori | 4. oto | 7. rea |
| 2. arl | 5. gig | 8. ark |
| 3. hoo | 6. dol | 9. tal |

## Newsroom Knowledge, page 16

1. Five
2. The Cincinnati Register
3. Three
4. February
5. Yellow
6. Franklin Roosevelt
7. Two

## Kirsten's New Name, page 16

Yellow Hair

## The Dancing Lesson, page 17

1. father
2. curtsy
3. gown
4. practice
5. bath
6. brushed
7. earrings
8. escort
9. manners

## Oh, Brothers!, page 18

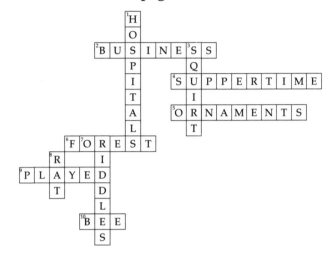

## City Search, page 20

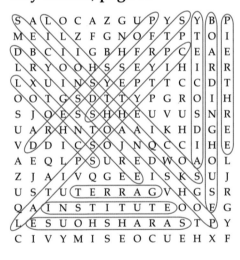

## A Surprise Friend, page 22

Jiggy Nye

## Celilo Falls, page 23

1. trading
2. games
3. dancing
4. races
5. parades
6. feasting

## Kitchen Quiz, page 26

sugar canister    mixer

pot holders    blue plates
teakettle    plants
coffee cups    fruit

cookie jar    cookbooks

## Sweet Sombrita, page 26

Little Shadow

**Party Problem, page 27**
Eddie Ryland put salt in the
ice cream.

**Penny Pincher Puzzle, page 28**

1. party hats
2. fiddle
3. dance
4. darling
5. camera
6. hot dogs
7. necklaces
8. dandelion
9. eggs
10. lanterns

Waste not, want not.

**Kaya Learns a Lesson, page 30**
You have to respect the horse you
are riding.

**Patchwork Pictures, page 31**

**Holiday Hobbies, page 33**

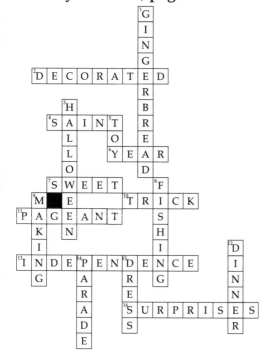

57

## Confused Keys, page 34
### (the changes are in red)

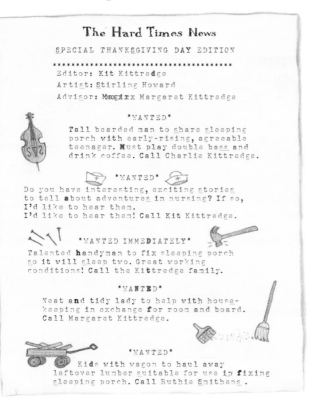

The Hard Times News

SPECIAL THANKSGIVING DAY EDITION

Editor: Kit Kittredge
Artist: Stirling Howard
Advisor: Margaret Margaret Kittredge

*WANTED*
Tall bearded man to share sleeping porch with early-rising, agreeable teenager. Must play double bass and drink coffee. Call Charlie Kittredge.

*WANTED*
Do you have interesting, exciting stories to tell about adventures in nursing? If so, I'd like to hear them.
I'd like to hear them! Call Kit Kittredge.

*WANTED IMMEDIATELY*
Talented handyman to fix sleeping porch so it will sleep two. Great working conditions! Call the Kittredge family.

*WANTED*
Neat and tidy lady to help with housekeeping in exchange for room and board. Call Margaret Kittredge.

*WANTED*
Kids with wagon to haul away leftover lumber suitable for use in fixing sleeping porch. Call Ruthie Smithens.

## Mr. Merriman's Shop, page 36

## Treasures to Trade, page 39
- a mirror
- knitting needles
- a toy farm

## Miss Victory, page 41

58